Angles of Achievement

Kristy Stark

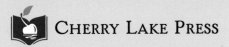

Published in the United States of America by Cherry Lake Publishing Group
Ann Arbor, Michigan
www.cherrylakepublishing.com

Reading Adviser: Beth Walker Gambro, MS, Ed., Reading Consultant, Yorkville, IL

Photo Credits: Cover: ©Boblgum / Getty Images; ©kapona / Shutterstock; ©Parinya Panyana / Shuttersock; ©fitie / Getty Images; ©kb-stocks / Getty Images; ©Olga Streinikova / Getty Images; page 5: ©Jessica Orozco; page 7: ©Roi and Roi / Getty Images; page 7: ©ONYXprj / Getty Images; page 8: ©Glam-Y / Getty Images; page 9: ©nuiiun / Getty Images; page 9: ©bortonia / Getty Images; page 9: ©bortonia / Getty Images; page 9: ©bortonia / Getty Images; page 10: ©Rudzhan Nagiev / Getty Images; page 11: ©photosynthesis / Getty Images; page 11: ©eestingnef / Getty Images; page 13: ©Jessica Orozco; page 14: ©Jessica Orozco; page 16: ©microgen / Getty Images; page 19: ©GoodStudio / Shutterstock; page 19: ©aleksandr-mansurov-ru / Getty Images; page 21: ©Jessica Orozco; page 22: ©Jessica Orozco; page 23: ©Jessica Orozc ; page 23: ©David W. Leindecker / Shutterstock; page 25: ©Jessica Orozco; page 26: ©Yuliyan Velchev / Shutterstock; page 26: ©Creativika Graphics / Shutterstock

Cherry Lake Press is an imprint of Cherry Lake Publishing Group.

Library of Congress Cataloging-in-Publication Data
Library of Congress Cataloging-in-Publication Data has been filed and is available at catalog.loc.gov.

Cherry Lake Publishing Group would like to acknowledge the work of the Partnership for 21st Century Learning, a Network of Battelle for Kids. Please visit http://www.battelleforkids.org/networks/p21 for more information.

Printed in the United States of America

Note from publisher: Websites change regularly, and their future contents are outside of our control. Supervise children when conducting any recommended online searches for extended learning opportunities.

Kristy Stark writes books about a variety of topics, from sports to biographies to science topics. When she is not busy writing, she enjoys reading, camping, lounging at the beach, and doing just about anything outdoors. Most of all, she loves to spend time with her husband, daughter, son, and two lazy cats at their home in Southern California.

CONTENTS

Angles and Arcs in Sports

Angles and arcs are all around us. From buildings to cars to books, a person can find an angle or arc. But did you know that angles and arcs can be found in sports, too? They are on the equipment players use. They make up the fields athletes play on. A player's body can even form angles and arcs as they play their sport and move their body on the court.

So what are angles and arcs? Angles are formed where two lines meet. Arcs are curved lines. These curves form a part of a circle.

Angles and Arcs All Around

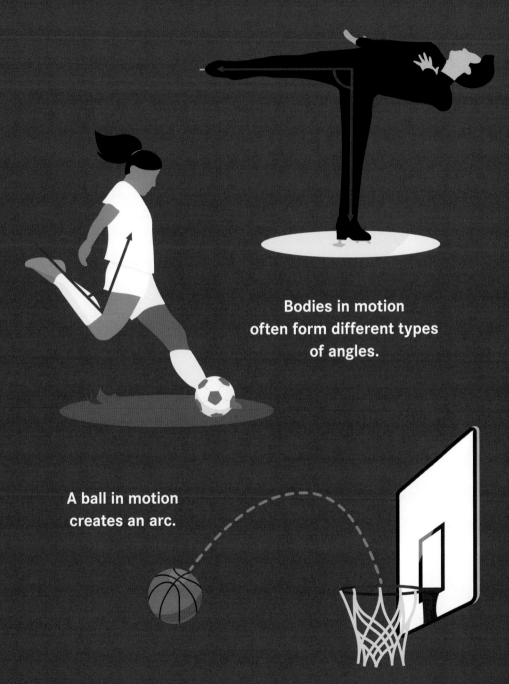

Bodies in motion
often form different types
of angles.

A ball in motion
creates an arc.

CHAPTER 1

Static Angles

An angle is the space formed when two lines or surfaces meet each other. Some angles change as an athlete moves or performs. Think about the angles of an athlete's legs. The angles change as they move. Other angles are **static**. This means that they do not change as the sport is played. Think of the angles formed by the lines on a balance beam. The lines do not move or change during the gymnastics routine. So the angles are static.

Static Versus Dynamic Angles

STATIC

DYNAMIC

Dynamic angles are angles that change as an athlete moves or performs.

How to Measure Angles

Angles are measured in **degrees** (°). They are measured with a tool called a **protractor**. Angles are measured from 0° to 180°. The tool has the degree marked on it.

3 Follow the other leg of the angle up to the top of the protractor to find the measurement. This angle measures 60°.

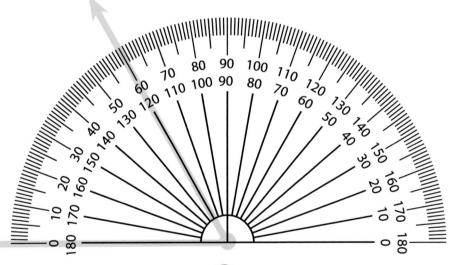

2 Line one leg of the angle up with the bottom edge of the protractor.

1 Find the middle of the protractor's bottom edge. Place it over the center point of the angle.

Right Angles

Right angles form where two lines meet at 90°. A square has four right angles, one in each corner.

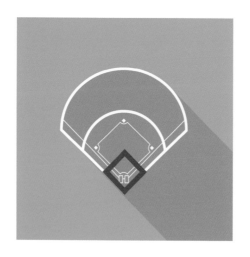

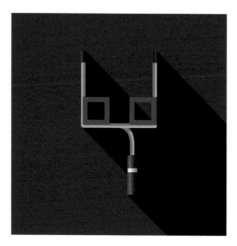

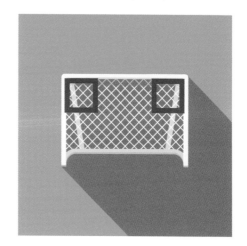

Acute Angles

Acute angles measure less than 90°. Acute means "sharp." These angles get their name because they form sharp points where the lines meet.

FAST FACTS

- Different types of skateboard ramps have different angles.
- Kicker ramps have a **slope** of 15° to 30°.
- Launch ramps are 60° or less. These ramps create a steep drop for riders.
- Quarter pipes have close to a 90° angle. As riders reach the top of the ramp, the front of their board points straight up!

Obtuse Angles

Obtuse angles measure more than 90°. But they are less than 180°.

Mixed martial arts (MMA) is a combat sport. Athletes can fight in Ultimate Fighting Championship (UFC) events. Each side of a UFC Octagon ring is an obtuse angle.

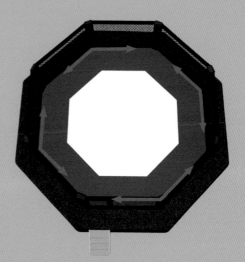

CHAPTER 2

Active Arcs

Angles are formed where two line segments meet. But arcs are curved lines. Picture a circle. An arc is a section of that circle.

Athletes often move their bodies in arcs rather than in straight lines. Think of a dancer as she leaps in the air. Her body follows an arc rather than a straight line. Her arms and legs form arcs, too. Imagine if dancers only moved in straight lines and angles. They would look more like robots! Dancers would be far less graceful without arcs.

Graceful Arcs

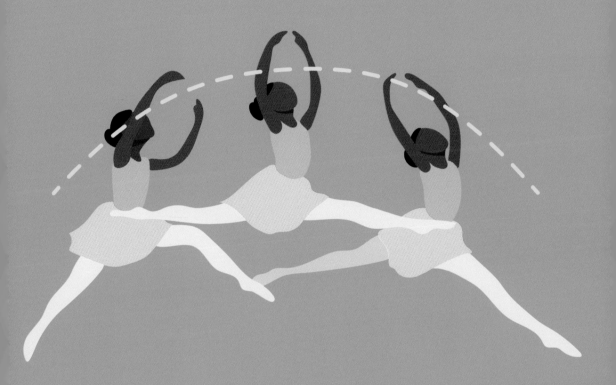

During the grand jeté, dancers raise their arms and pull up their legs. They look almost as if they were floating through the air. But really, their bodies are following a curved arc.

Imagine a quarterback's arm as he throws the ball. His arm follows an arc. The ball follows an arc, too. Long, deep passes have high arcs. Short, close passes have low arcs.

Deep Passes Make High Arcs

One deep pass is the Hail Mary. To make a Hail Mary, the player takes a step back and then forward to give the throw more speed. They throw the ball over their head and release it early to create a high arc.

Short Passes Make Low Arcs

A bullet pass is a short pass. The player snaps their arm forward quickly. They throw the ball next to their head and release it late to create a low arc. A bullet pass is fast and short-range.

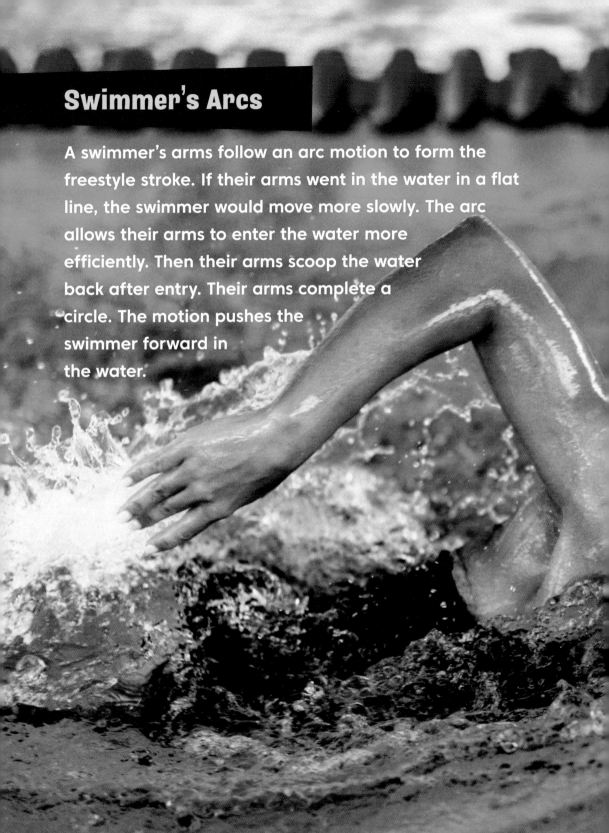

Swimmer's Arcs

A swimmer's arms follow an arc motion to form the freestyle stroke. If their arms went in the water in a flat line, the swimmer would move more slowly. The arc allows their arms to enter the water more efficiently. Then their arms scoop the water back after entry. Their arms complete a circle. The motion pushes the swimmer forward in the water.

CHAPTER 3

Angles to Achieve an Edge

Angles can play a huge role in an athlete's performance. In fact, angles are so important that Major League Baseball (MLB) tracks stats about them. It tracks the **launch angle** for different types of contact with the ball. The launch angle is the **vertical** angle at which the ball leaves the bat.

- Ground ball: less than 10°
- Line drive: 10° to 25°
- Fly ball: 25° to 50°
- Pop-up: greater than 50°

Launch Angles

Pop-Up

50°

Fly Ball

25°

Line Drive

10°

0°

Ground Ball

2022, MLB Glossary; 2021, V1 Sports Blog

Pitchers want to control their launch angles. When they do, they have greater control over pitch location. They can pitch more balls within the **strike zone**.

Approximate Launch Angle by Pitch Height

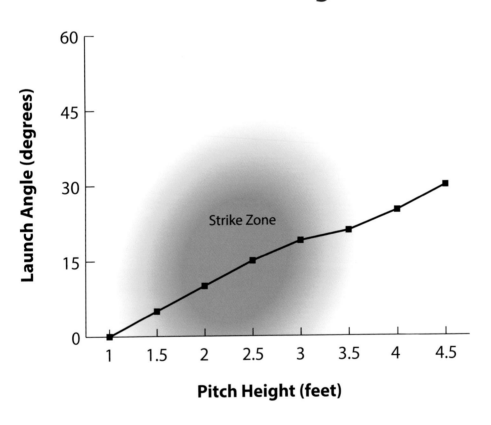

2020, Six Man Rotation

Connecting with the Ball

In baseball, the angle with which the bat connects with the ball makes a huge difference. Players hit more home runs when the bat hits the ball at an angle of 8° to 32°. This angle yields a greater chance of an **exit velocity** of 95 miles per hour (mph) or higher.

- Hit under: The bat connects with the ball from 40° to 90°. This means the bat hits the underside of the ball. This likely results in a foul or fly ball.

- Topped: The bat connects with the ball at an angle of 0° and under. This means the bat hits the top of the ball. This usually results in a ground ball.

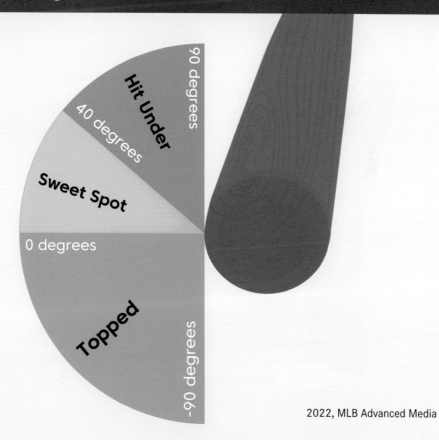

90 degrees

Hit Under

40 degrees

Sweet Spot

0 degrees

Topped

-90 degrees

2022, MLB Advanced Media

The angle of a golfer's stance is key to hitting the ball with **accuracy**. It is best to hold the upper body at a 40° to 45° angle. This improves the golfer's arm position. And that helps their swing.

40° to 45°

25°

9°

2017, Westridge Golf Centre

Tiger Woods is one of history's best golf players. Scientists analyzed the angles and arcs of his play during his peak years.

Woods aims his putter 2.5° to the right of the start line.

His putting stroke moves upward by about 2.4° during the stroke but hits the ball straight-on.

His entire putting stroke creates more of an arc than other players— about 20°.

2019, EB Golf Media

CHAPTER 4

Breaking Records

An athlete's technique and speed are important. These features help them perform their best. At times, the first few fractions of a second can make or break an athlete's chances of winning.

For sprinters, a good start is a key factor to win the race. They need to respond quickly to the starting gun. They also need to get out of the starting blocks before the other runners. A good angle can boost a sprinter's acceleration.

Acceleration Angle

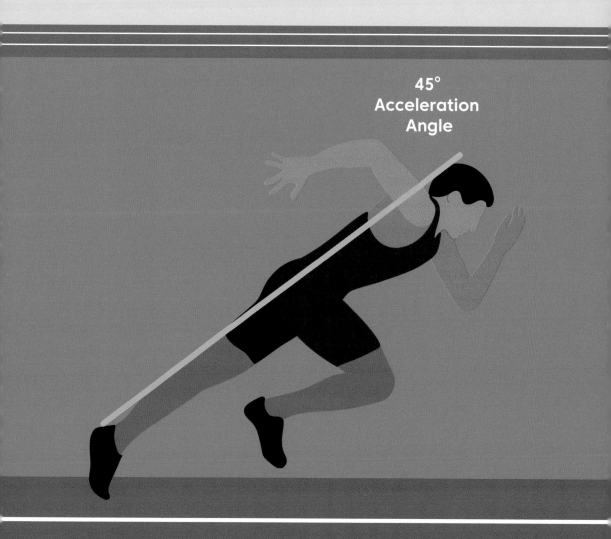

45°
Acceleration
Angle

The History of 100-Meter Dash Times (Women)

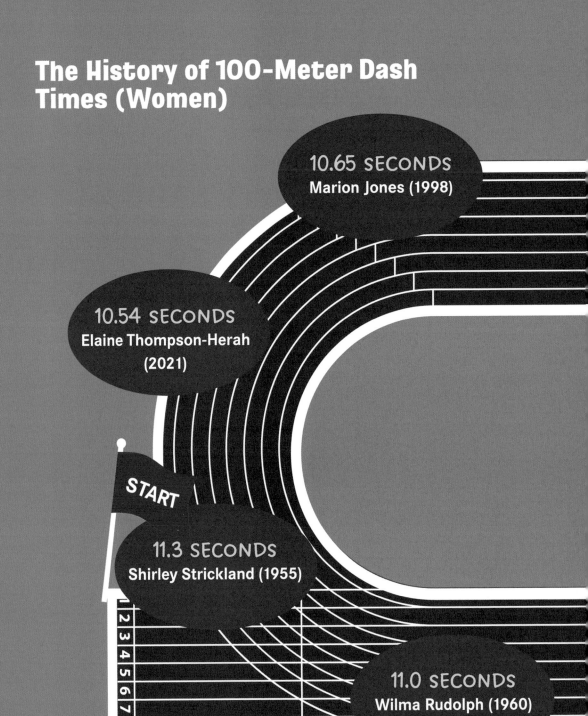

10.65 SECONDS
Marion Jones (1998)

10.54 SECONDS
Elaine Thompson-Herah (2021)

START

11.3 SECONDS
Shirley Strickland (1955)

11.0 SECONDS
Wilma Rudolph (1960)

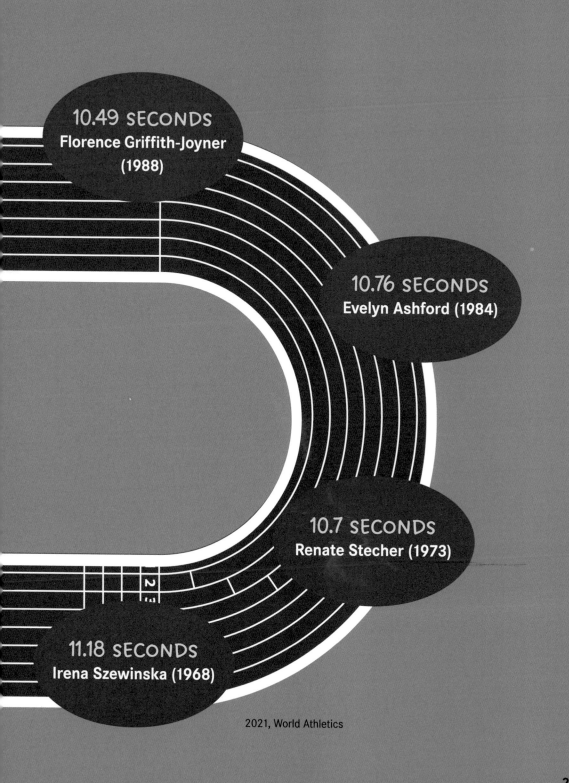

10.49 SECONDS
Florence Griffith-Joyner (1988)

10.76 SECONDS
Evelyn Ashford (1984)

10.7 SECONDS
Renate Stecher (1973)

11.18 SECONDS
Irena Szewinska (1968)

2021, World Athletics

Men's Running World Records by Athlete's Country

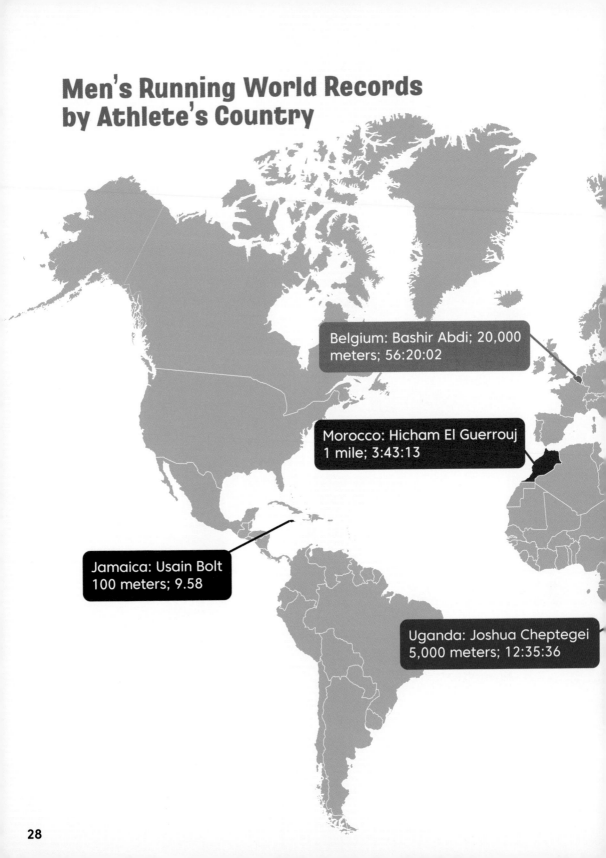

Belgium: Bashir Abdi; 20,000 meters; 56:20:02

Morocco: Hicham El Guerrouj 1 mile; 3:43:13

Jamaica: Usain Bolt 100 meters; 9.58

Uganda: Joshua Cheptegei 5,000 meters; 12:35:36

Russia: Wayde Van Niekerk
400 meters; 43.03

Kenya: David Rudisha
800 meters; 1:40:91

Kenya: Noah Ngeny
1,000 meters; 2:11:96

2021, World Athletics

Activity

Angle Adventure

Now you know all about angles in sports. It's time to measure angles on some of your favorite players or athletes. Picture the way these athletes move their bodies. Imagine all those angles!

Choose three to five players you want to measure.

MATERIALS NEEDED
- Magazines or computer and printer
- Scissors and glue
- Paper or poster board
- Writing utensil and highlighter
- Protractor

1. Find images of these athletes in magazines or on websites. Print or cut out the images. Glue them onto chart paper or poster board.

2. Highlight one angle on the athlete's body. Use a protractor to measure that angle. If you do not have a protractor, you can find an online protractor and use it to estimate the angle.

3. Label each highlighted angle with the measurement.

Want to measure more angles? Move your body into different angles. Have a family member or friend take a picture of you in each position. Then print the pictures and glue them to paper. Repeat the steps above to measure your angles.

Learn More

Books

Buckley, James Jr. *It's a Numbers Game! Soccer: The Math Behind the Perfect Goal, the Game-Winning Save, and So Much More!* Washington, DC: National Geographic Kids, 2020.

Ventura, Marne. *Learning STEM from Baseball*. New York: Sky Pony, 2020.

Wall, Julie. *Basketball Angles*. Huntington Beach, CA: Teacher Created Materials, 2009.

Online Resources to Explore with an Adult

Our Family Code: Measure Athlete Angles in Olympic Sports

PBS Kids: The Science of Angles: Learn Through Sports

Bibliography

Math Is Fun. Names of Angles. September 22, 2001.

Measurement of Angles. Encyclopedia.com.

MLB Glossary. February 4, 2020.

World Athletics. Records by Event. February 2021.

Glossary

acceleration (ak-sell-uh-RAY-shun) the act of moving faster

accuracy (AK-yuhr-uh-see) freedom from mistake or error

acute angles (uh-KYOOT ANG-uhls) angles that measure less than 90°

degrees (duh-GREES) units for measuring the size of an angle

dynamic (dai-NA-mik) constantly active or changing

exit velocity (EG-zit vuh-LOSS-uh-tee) a measurement of the speed of a baseball as it comes off the bat

launch angle (LAWNCH ANG-uhl) the vertical angle at which a ball leaves a player's bat after being struck

obtuse angles (OB-toos ANG-uhls) angles that measure more than 90° but less than 180°

protractor (proh-TRAK-tur) a tool used to measure angles

right angles (RITE ANg-uhls) angles that measure 90°

slope (SLOHP) a downward slant

sprinters (SPRIN-turs) runners who race over a short distance at a very fast speed

static (STAH-tik) showing little or no change or action

strike zone (STRYKE ZOHN) the area over home plate from the midpoint between a batter's shoulders and the top of the uniform pants

technique (tek-NEEK) a way of doing something that uses special knowledge or skill

vertical (VER-tuh-kuhl) positioned up and down; going straight up

Index